A Note to Parents

DK READERS is a compelling program for beginning readers, designed in conjunction with leading literacy experts, including Dr. Linda Gambrell, Director of the Eugene T. Moore School of Education at Clemson University. Dr. Gambrell has served on the Board of Directors of the International Reading Association and as President of the National Reading Conference.

Beautiful illustrations and superb full-color photographs combine with engaging, easy-to-read stories to offer a fresh approach to each subject in the series. Each DK READER is guaranteed to capture a child's interest while developing his or her reading skills, general knowledge, and love of reading.

The five levels of DK READERS are aimed at different reading abilities, enabling you to choose the books that are exactly right for your child:

Pre-level 1: Learning to read
Level 1: Beginning to read
Level 2: Beginning to read alone
Level 3: Reading alone
Level 4: Proficient readers

The "normal" age at which a child begins to read can be anywhere from three to eight years old, so these levels are only a general guideline.

No matter which level you select, you can be sure that you are helping your child learn to read, then read to learn!

DK

LONDON, NEW YORK, MUNICH,
MELBOURNE, AND DELHI

Series Editor Deborah Lock
Designer Sadie Thomas
U.S. Editor Elizabeth Hester
Production Alison Lenane
DTP Designer Almudena Díaz
and Pilar Morales
Jacket Designer Simon Oon

Reading Consultant
Linda Gambrell, Ph.D.

First American Edition, 2004
12 13 14 15 14
Published in the United States by DK Publishing, Inc.
375 Hudson Street, New York, New York 10014
023-AD167-Oct/2004
Copyright © 2004 Dorling Kindersley Limited

Published in Great Britain by Dorling Kindersley Limited

Library of Congress Cataloging-in-Publication Data
Farm animals.-- 1st American ed.
    p. cm. -- (DK readers, pre-level 1)
ISBN 978-0-7566-0536-0 (pbk)   ISBN 978-0-7566-0534-6 (hbk)
1. Livestock--Juvenile literature. I. Dorling Kindersley readers. Pre-level
1, Learning to read.
SF75.5.F367 2004
636--dc22
                                                        2004007457

6902

Color reproduction by Colourscan, Singapore
Printed and bound in China by L Rex Printing Co., Ltd.

The publisher would like to thank the following for their kind
permission to reproduce their photographs:
a=above; c=center; b=below; l=left; r=right t=top:

www.agripicture.com: Peter Dean 22–23. **Alamy Images:** Bildagentur
Geduldig/archivberlin Fotoagentur GmbH 18-19; Jack Sullivan 26-27.
Ardea.com: John Daniels 10-11. **Corbis:** Darrell Gulin 8-9; Kit Houghton
24-25; Randy M. Ury 4-5. **DK Picture Library:** Barleylands Farm Museum
and Animal Centre 6, 8–9, 16; Philip Dowell 12, 14, 15, 18; Jerry Young
15; Tracy Morgan 15; Odds Farm Park 19; Barrie Watts 20, 21.
Getty Images: Pal Hermansen 20t; Hans Reinhard 11t. **Holt Studios
International:** 15t. **Oxford Scientific Films:** Mark Hamblin 14-15;
Konrad Wothe 12t.

All other images © Dorling Kindersley
For further information see: www.dkimages.com

Discover more at
www.dk.com

DK READERS

LEARNING
pre-level
1
TO READ

Farm Animals

DK Publishing, Inc.

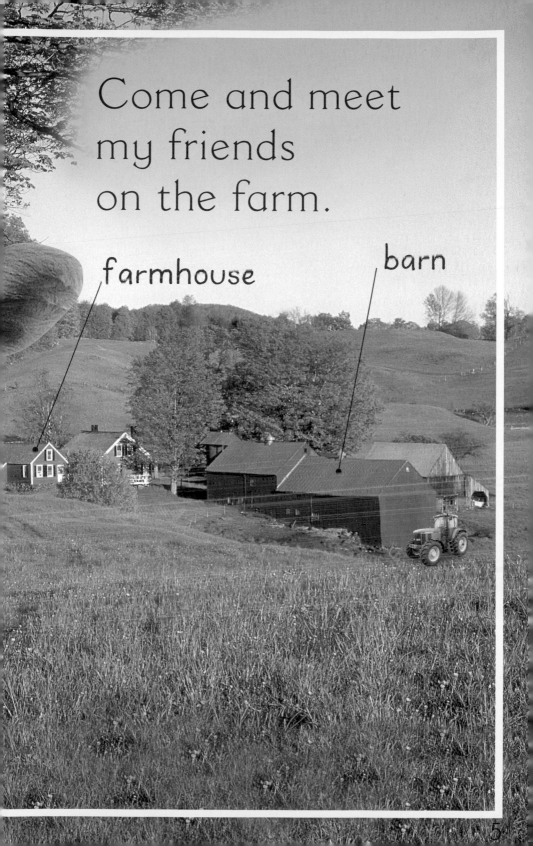

Come and meet
my friends
on the farm.

farmhouse

barn

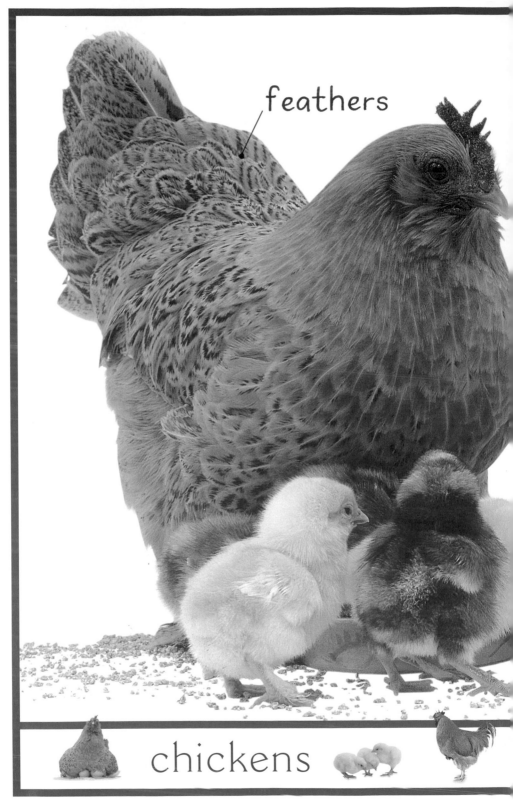

feathers

chickens

Here is the chicken
with her little chicks.

chick

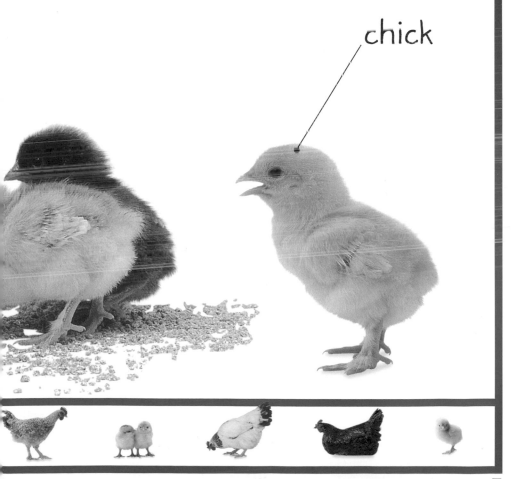

Here is the turkey coming to meet you.

beak

 turkeys

feathers

Here is the pig.
Here are three
pink piglets.

piglet

 pigs

ear

Here are the cows looking at you.

hoof_____

 COWS

udder

calf

13

Here is the dog.
Here are three
sleepy puppies.

nose

puppy

dogs

Here are the sheep with a little lamb.

lamb

sheep

wool

ear

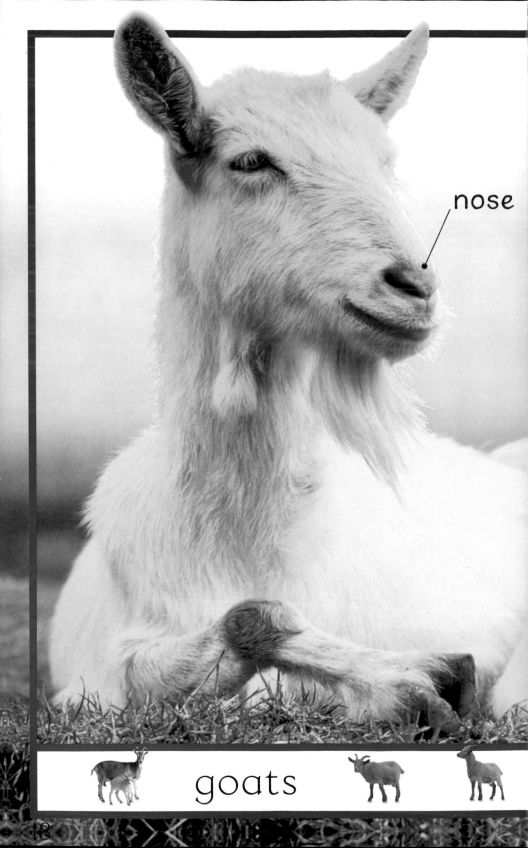

nose

goats

Here is the goat
lying down
with her kid.

kid

Here are the ducks
with their
fluffy ducklings.

   ducks

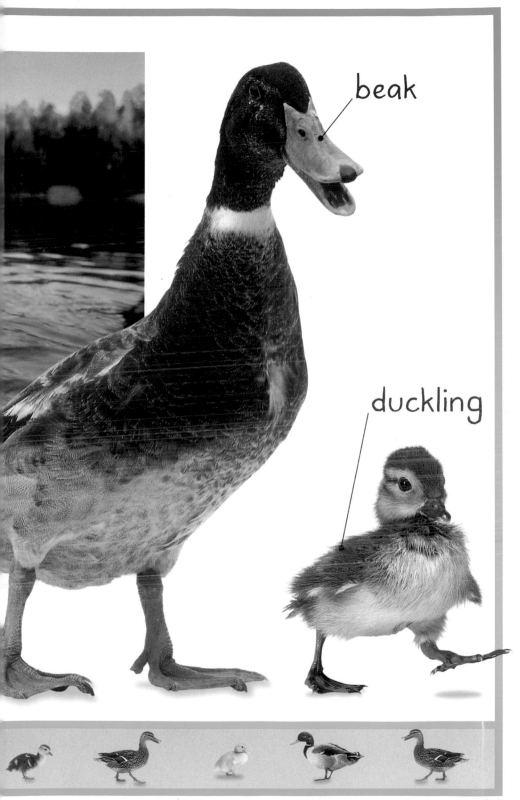

beak

duckling

21

Here are
the white geese
looking all around.

 geese

eye

neck

Here is the horse running with her foal.

foal

horses

mane

ponies

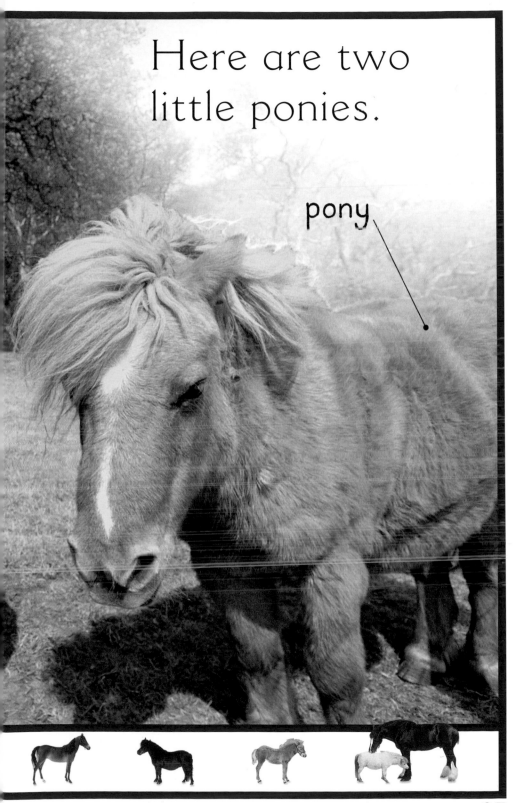

Here are two little ponies.

pony

Here is the cat
curled up with
her kitten.

kitten

 cats

hay

ear

29

Come see us again soon!

Moo!

Which animals

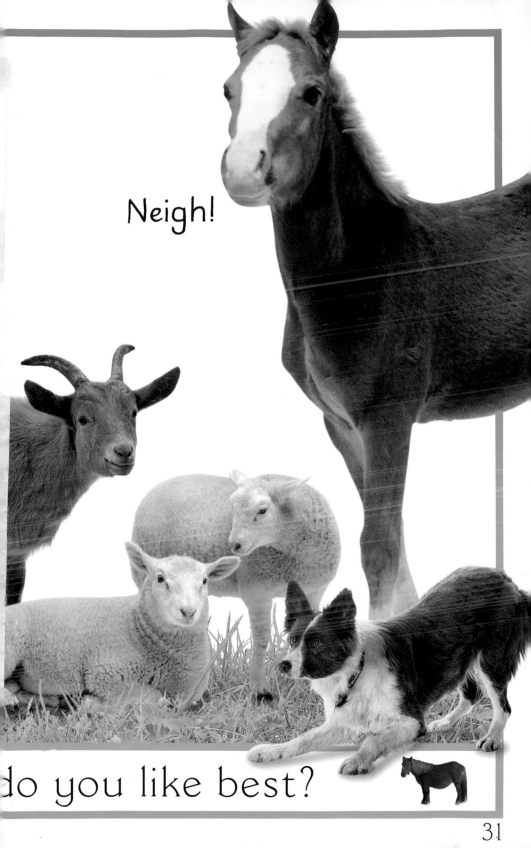

Neigh!

do you like best?

Picture word list

chicken
page 6

turkey
page 8

pig
page 10

cow
page 12

dog
page 14

sheep
page 16

goat
page 18

duck
page 20

goose
page 22

horse
page 24

pony
page 26

cat
page 28